COOKING

THE

RUSSIAN

WAY

Lerner Publications Company
A division of Lerner Publishing Group
241 First Avenue North
Minneapolis, MN 55401 U.S.A.

Website address: www.lernerbooks.com

Library of Congress Cataloging-in-Publication Data

Plotkin, Gregory.
    Cooking the Russian way / by Gregory and Rita Plotkin—Rev. &
expanded.
        p.   cm. — (Easy menu ethnic cookbooks)
    Includes index.
    Summary: Introduces the cooking and food habits of Russia, including
such recipes as beet soup or borsch, stuffed pastries or pirozhki, and beef
Stroganoff; also provides brief information on the geography and history
of the country.
    ISBN: 0–8225–4120–3 (lib. bdg. : alk. paper)
    1. Cookery, Russian—Juvenile literature. 2. Russia (Federation)—
Social life and customs—Juvenile literature. [1. Cookery, Russian. 2.
Russia (Federation)—Social life and customs.] I. Plotkin, Rita. II. Title.
III. Series.
TX723.3 .P58 2003
641.5947—dc21   2001008163

Manufactured in the United States of America
1 2 3 4 5 6 – JR – 08 07 06 05 04 03

easy menu ethnic cookbooks

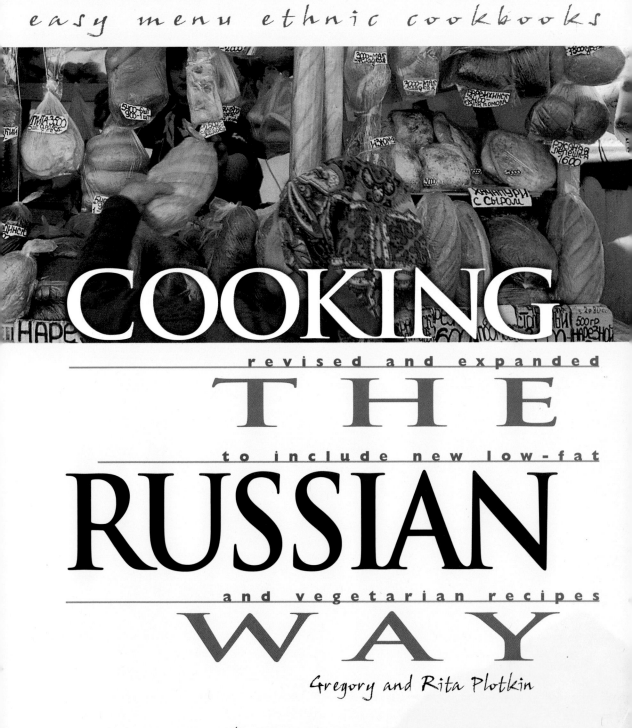

COOKING

revised and expanded

THE

to include new low-fat

RUSSIAN

and vegetarian recipes

WAY

Gregory and Rita Plotkin

Lerner Publications Company • Minneapolis

Contents

Introduction

Russia is a country of enormous proportions, from its vast forests to its long history. It is also a country of enormous diversity, with a great variety of landscapes, cultures, and traditions. These factors have helped to produce a unique cuisine.

Russians love to eat, and Russian cooks are proud of their specialties. Although food has not always been plentiful in this land of wide expanses and long winters, gourmet chefs and grandmothers alike have learned to use the resources at hand to create tempting dishes. In the winter, potatoes, root vegetables, and hearty breads provide hot, filling meals. Russia's seas and long rivers offer a plentiful supply of fish, and Russian cooks also make good use of meat and dairy products in their dishes. Fresh fruits and vegetables are savored in the summer and are carefully preserved to be enjoyed when cold weather arrives. From refreshing cold salads to steaming hot blini, the cuisine of Russia is as varied and interesting as it is delicious.

Borsch (beet soup) is a Russian classic that adds color to any table. (Recipe on page 40.)

The Land

Russia stretches across eastern Europe and northern and central Asia. It is the largest country in the world—more than one and a half times the size of the United States—and many different landscapes and climates exist within its boundaries. Parts of northern Russia reach above the Arctic Circle and do not see the sun for six months of the year, while balmy southern regions almost never have snow.

Located on the European Plain, western Russia is the country's most well developed and populous area. Except for the Caucasus Mountains in the south, the region is made up of flat plains and low hills. The Volga River runs southward through the region to the Caspian Sea, and the area contains most of the country's major cities, including Moscow (the national capital) and Saint Petersburg. The western plains are also home to most of Russia's industries.

Separating European Russia from Asian Russia, the Ural Mountains run the length of the country from north to south. East of the Urals lies wintry Siberia, a huge; sparsely populated area that stretches to Russia's eastern seacoast. Siberia is divided into the West Siberian Plain, the Central Siberian Plateau, and the East Siberian Uplands. Siberia is also divided into several different zones based on climate. The far northern reaches of Siberia are tundra—a harsh, cold zone in which much of the land is permanently frozen. South of the tundra is the taiga, a vast forested region. Still farther south lies the steppe, a wide grassland that contains Russia's most fertile soil. Siberia is watered by the Ob, Yenisei, and Lena Rivers along with other smaller waterways. Lake Baikal, in south-central Siberia, is the world's deepest freshwater lake.

The History

Russia's history spans more than one thousand years. An ethnic group called the Slavs began to settle in the region in about the A.D. 500s. The Slavs established the first Russian state, called Rus, during the 800s. Internal unrest and foreign invasions troubled the young nation for centuries. But in 1547, Ivan IV—also known as Ivan the Terrible—became the first of a series of powerful leaders called czars who would rule Russia for almost four hundred years. The czars gradually purchased and conquered territory until, by the reign of Peter the Great in the late 1600s and early 1700s, Russia had grown into a large and powerful nation.

The 1800s were a time of great political unrest in Russia. The

Built between 1754 and 1762, Saint Petersburg's majestic Winter Palace became a state museum in 1917.

workers and the middle class were unhappy with their terrible working conditions and the extreme inequalities in Russian society. In January 1905, workers made a peaceful march on Czar Nicholas II's Winter Palace in Saint Petersburg to demand reform. The czar's troops fired on the crowd, killing and wounding hundreds of people. Violence broke out all over the country as Russians protested this massacre, which came to be known as Bloody Sunday. The czar was forced to agree to some reforms, including the establishment of an elected Duma, or parliament, but it wasn't enough to stop the brewing revolution.

In 1917 Nicholas II stepped down from the throne under heavy pressure from revolutionaries. A few months later, a group called the Bolsheviks, led by Vladimir Lenin, violently seized control of the nation. The Bolsheviks changed the group's name to the Communist Party Congress and established the Union of Soviet Socialist Republics (USSR), or Soviet Union, in 1922. The USSR eventually grew to include Russia and fourteen other republics. Under the control of the Communist Party, the USSR became one of the most powerful nations in the world.

After World War II (1939–1945), relations were strained between the Soviet Union and noncommunist nations such as the United States and its European allies. This period became known as the Cold War. The USSR's international relationships began to improve during the 1980s, but its internal stability weakened as republics within the USSR began to call for independence. By the end of 1991, the Soviet Union had collapsed, and Russia, officially called the Russian Federation, had become an independent nation once again.

The Food

Many traditional dishes in Russian cuisine are based on the simple but hearty cooking of the peasants of prerevolutionary Russia. Bread, a longtime staple, remains one of the most important and most loved foods in modern Russia. Borsch is another food that was handed down by the peasants. It is a soup made from beets and any of a variety of other ingredients, including cabbage, carrots, potatoes, onions, and meat.

Russian cooking also has roots in the food favored by the nobility of prerevolutionary Russia. The most striking characteristic of this cuisine was the amount of food served at one time. An upper-class dinner featured course after course of rich, delicious food, beginning with substantial *zakuski*, or appetizers. Zakuski were usually made up of a wide array of Russian foods, from pickled vegetables and caviar (fish eggs) to smoked fish and hot *pirozhki* (stuffed pastries). The main meal often included meat, poultry, and fish, as well as soup, salad, cooked vegetables, and a rich dessert. Although very few modern Russians eat on such a large scale, many traditional dishes, such as beef Stroganoff and Russian salad, are still favorites, and serving elaborate zakuski is still a popular custom.

A Russian shopper takes advantage of the fresh produce available at a local market.

Russian dining grew more diverse during the Soviet era, when many traditional foods from the other republics of the USSR became favorites of Russian cooks. The former southern republics of Armenia and Georgia, for example, contributed chickpeas, pine nuts, and cracked wheat to the national cuisine. Typical dishes such as *shashlyk* (grilled lamb on skewers), dolmas (grape leaves stuffed with rice and meat), and baklava (a rich pastry made with honey and nuts) also made their way into Russian cooking.

Farther east, the former republics in central Asia, such as Uzbekistan and Turkmenistan, introduced *plov*, a mixture of rice, lamb, and spices that is similar to the pilafs served in the Middle East. Diners in Russia soon included many of these tasty treats on their own menus. A wealth of delicious fruit, including figs, grapes, peaches, apples, cherries, and melons, is also an important part of the cuisine of this region.

After the fall of the Soviet Union, foods and restaurants from Europe and the United States also appeared in Russia. But Russia's traditional cuisine is still served every day by native cooks, and with the recipes in this book you can prepare some of these delicious classics yourself. You're sure to love the many flavors of this vast and varied country.

Holidays and Festivals

The Russian fondness for food is especially apparent during holidays and festivals. These occasions give friends and family the perfect excuse to gather for reunions, parties, and special meals, and Russian cooks prepare delicacies to satisfy even the most robust appetites.

Most Russians belong to the Russian Orthodox Church, a branch of Eastern Orthodox Christianity, and observe church holidays throughout the year. In ancient Russia, many festivals were held in honor of nature, the seasons, and the harvests. When the Orthodox religion took hold in Russia in the A.D. 900s, many features of the old festivals were incorporated into church celebrations. During the Soviet era, the government discouraged church holidays and worship, but many people in the USSR adapted celebrations of national and political holidays to include some of their treasured religious traditions. In modern-day Russia, people are once again allowed to celebrate religious holidays, and their customs combine the heritage of the past with modern practices.

Easter, or Paskha, is by far the most important holiday on the Orthodox calendar. Easter Sunday usually falls sometime around April, but the holiday season begins much earlier. During Lent, the period before Easter, most Russian Orthodox Christians fast, excluding meat and dairy products from their diets. To prepare for Lent, Russians celebrate Maslenitsa, also called Butter Week or Pancake Week. Held the week before Lent begins, this festival is a time for sleigh rides, bonfires—and lots of eating. The traditional treats for Maslenitsa are blini, thin pancakes served with plenty of butter. Other favorite toppings include caviar, smoked fish, sour cream, and jam. In ancient times, this carnival-like holiday also represented the coming of the end of winter. Burning a scarecrow in a bonfire was a popular custom, representing the heat of the sun melting the snow and ice of winter.

As Easter draws near, Russian cooks spend as long as a week preparing a feast for the occasion. Two special desserts, the kulich (a tall, sweet bread made with nuts and dried fruit and topped with a white glaze or frosting) and the paskha (a rich cheesecake, traditionally formed into a pyramid shape) appear at almost every family's Easter dinner. These and other sweets are set out on the table the night before Easter, along with a tempting array of cold appetizers and main courses. Blini, cheese, cold meats, and smoked fish may be just a few of the choices. The traditional Easter table also displays flowers and greenery, bowls of hard-cooked, decorated eggs, and a figure of a lamb made of molded butter.

Near midnight, Russians head to church to attend Easter Mass. Many cooks bring along the kulich, paskha, and other items of the

A Russian Orthodox priest blesses food for an Easter meal.

next day's meal to be blessed by the priest. The long church service reaches its climax when the priest carries a cross down the aisle and out the church doors. The congregation follows, singing, and the procession circles the building three times. At last Easter has begun. Family and friends offer each other the customary Easter greeting of three kisses on alternate cheeks and hurry home, eager to begin the feast that awaits them. Hot dishes such as spicy sausage, roast lamb, veal, or ham are added to the spread already laid out on the table, and everyone digs in.

In the Orthodox calendar, the first day of the new year, January 1, comes before Christmas, which falls on January 7. During the years of Soviet rule, New Year's celebrations absorbed many Russian Orthodox Christmas traditions, and the new year continues to be a bigger and more festive holiday than Christmas in many modern-day Russian homes. Many families decorate a pine tree with ornaments and candles. Grandfather Frost and the Snow Maiden visit households on New Year's Eve, leaving gifts and goodies for children. Adults celebrate the occasion with parties and special delicacies, and on New Year's Day families gather around the table for a big holiday dinner.

Christmas (Rozhdestvo) is celebrated a week later, beginning on Christmas Eve. For many families, the only meal of the day follows the Christmas Eve church service. This special late-evening dinner is usually meatless, but as many as twelve delicious courses of vegetables, grains, and fish may be served. A special favorite is kutya, a dish made with steamed, sweetened wheat mixed with raisins and nuts. Families attend church again on Christmas morning, often bringing fresh branches of cherry blossoms, grown from indoor trees, to adorn the icons (religious paintings). Back at home, families sit down to share another large meal. Like the Easter dinner, this meal breaks a fast. For the first time in four weeks, meat and dairy are part of the menu, and at least one main dish of pork, goose, duck, turkey, or chicken is usually on the table. Pirozhki and pelmeni (stuffed dumplings) are also common Christmas dishes. The decorated tree is still in place for everyone to admire, and groups of carolers go from house to house, sharing songs and snacking on sweets offered by their hosts and hostesses. Sleigh rides, dancing, and fortune-telling are other popular pastimes during the Christmas holiday.

Russia also has populations of Jews and Muslims, who, like Christians, have more freedom to celebrate religious holidays than they did during the Soviet era. The Jewish holiday of Passover falls in March or April. Russian Jews observe the traditional Passover meal with dishes such as matzo (a special unleavened bread), chicken pilaf with apples, and gefilte fish (patties of chopped fish with onions). Russian Muslims fast between sunrise and sunset during Ramadan, the holiest month of the Islamic year. The dates of Ramadan change each year, but the end of the month is always celebrated with Eid al-Fitr, a great feast for which cooks prepare an array of tasty rice, vegetable, and meat dishes.

Russians around the country also mark seasonal festivals and events. In ancient Russia, one celebration honored the return of skylarks from their winter migration, a sure sign of spring. People sang songs to welcome the birds, and cooks baked sweet rolls in the shape of larks. Although few people observe the festival anymore, Russians with a sweet tooth can often find the rolls in their local bakeries around March. In the countryside, many rural villages observe agricultural celebrations, from apple and honey harvests to festivals in honor of the local livestock. Throughout the year, and all around the nation of Russia, people come together to mark special occasions with friends, family, and food.

Russians brave the chilly weather to celebrate an ancient festival of spring.

Before You Begin

Russian cooking makes use of some ingredients that you may not know. Sometimes special cookware is used, too, although the recipes in this book can be prepared with ordinary utensils and pans.

The most important thing you need to know before you start is how to be a careful cook. On the following page, you'll find a few rules that will make your cooking experience safe, fun, and easy. Next, take a look at the "dictionary" of utensils, terms, and special ingredients. You may also want to read the list of tips on preparing healthy, low-fat meals.

When you've picked out a recipe to try, read through it from beginning to end. Now you are ready to shop for ingredients and to organize the cookware you will need. Once you have assembled everything, you're ready to begin cooking.

The tall, frosted kulich is a must for a traditional Russian Easter dinner. (Recipe on pages 64–65.)

The Careful Cook

Whenever you cook, there are certain safety rules you must always keep in mind. Even experienced cooks follow these rules when they are in the kitchen.

- Always wash your hands before handling food. Thoroughly wash all raw vegetables and fruits to remove dirt, chemicals, and insecticides. Wash uncooked poultry, fish, and meat under cold water.
- Use a cutting board when cutting up vegetables and fruits. Don't cut them up in your hand! And be sure to cut in a direction *away* from you and your fingers.
- Long hair or loose clothing can easily catch fire if brought near the burners of a stove. If you have long hair, tie it back before you start cooking.
- Turn all pot handles toward the back of the stove so that you will not catch your sleeves or jewelry on them. This is especially important when younger brothers and sisters are around. They could easily knock off a pot and get burned.
- Always use a pot holder to steady hot pots or to take pans out of the oven. Don't use a wet cloth on a hot pan because the steam it produces could burn you.
- Lift the lid of a steaming pot with the opening away from you so that you will not get burned.
- If you get burned, hold the burn under cold running water. Do not put grease or butter on it. Cold water helps to take the heat out, but grease or butter will only keep it in.
- If grease or cooking oil catches fire, throw baking soda or salt at the bottom of the flame to put it out. (Water will not put out a grease fire.) Call for help, and try to turn all the stove burners to "off."

Cooking Utensils

colander—A bowl with holes in the bottom and sides. It is used for draining liquid from a solid food.

Dutch oven—A heavy pot with a tight-fitting domed lid that is often used for cooking soups or stews

rolling pin—A cylindrical tool used for rolling out dough

slotted spoon—A spoon with small openings in the bowl. It is often used to remove solid food from a liquid.

spatula—A flat, thin utensil, usually metal, used to lift, toss, turn, or scoop up food

tongs—A utensil shaped either like tweezers or scissors with flat, blunt ends used to grasp food

whisk—A small wire utensil used for beating foods by hand

Cooking Terms

beat—To stir rapidly in a circular motion

boil—To heat a liquid over high heat until bubbles form and rise rapidly to the surface

fold—To blend an ingredient with other ingredients by using a gentle, overturning circular motion instead of by stirring or beating

garnish—To decorate a dish with small pieces of food such as parsley

grate—To cut food into small pieces by rubbing it against a grater

knead—To work dough by pressing it down in the center with both palms, pushing it outward, and then folding it over on itself and rotating the ball of dough before pressing down again

mince—To chop food into very small pieces

preheat—To allow an oven to warm up to a certain temperature before putting food in it

sauté—To fry quickly over high heat in oil or fat, stirring or turning the food to prevent burning

simmer—To cook over low heat in liquid kept just below its boiling point. Bubbles may occasionally rise to the surface.

steep—To soak a substance, such as tea, in hot water to extract flavor

Special Ingredients

bay leaf—The dried leaf of the bay (also called laurel) tree, used to season food

buttermilk—A milk product made from soured milk. Buttermilk is available in low-fat and skim varieties.

cardamom seed—A spice of the ginger family, used whole or ground, that has a rich aroma and gives food a sweet, cool taste

cinnamon—A spice made from the bark of a tree in the laurel family. Cinnamon is available ground and in sticks.

cornstarch—A fine, powdered white starch made from corn, commonly used for thickening sauces and gravies

corn syrup—A sweet syrup made from cornstarch

dill—An herb whose seeds and leaves are both used in cooking. Dried dill is also called dill weed.

farmer cheese—A white cheese made from whole or partially skimmed milk

feta cheese—A crumbly, white cheese made from goat's milk

Gruyère cheese—A firm white cheese from Switzerland that is often used in cooking and which melts very well

nutmeg—A fragrant spice, either whole or ground, that is often used in desserts

olive oil—An oil, made from pressed olives, that is used in cooking and for dressing salads *ricotta cheese*—A creamy white cheese that resembles cottage cheese. Ricotta is available in low-fat and skim varieties.

scallion—A variety of green onion

sunflower oil—A cooking oil made from sunflower seeds. Sunflower oil is especially popular in Russia, but vegetable oil or canola oil can be substituted.

wheat berries—whole kernels of wheat that have not been processed. Wheat berries are often sold in the health-food sections of supermarkets and also in specialty health-food stores.

yeast—An ingredient used in baking that causes dough to rise. Yeast is available in either small, white cakes called compressed yeast or in granular form called active dry yeast.

Healthy and Low-Fat Cooking Tips

Many modern cooks are concerned about preparing healthy, low-fat meals. Fortunately, there are simple ways to reduce the fat content of most dishes. Here are a few general tips for adapting the recipes in this book. Throughout the book, you'll also find specific suggestions for individual recipes—and don't worry, they'll still taste delicious!

Many recipes call for butter or oil to sauté some ingredients. Using oil instead of butter can lower cholesterol and saturated fat, but you can also reduce the amount of oil or use a low-fat or non-fat cooking spray instead of oil. Another common substitution for butter is margarine. Before making this substitution, consider the recipe. If it is a dessert, it's often best to use butter. Margarine may noticeably change the taste or consistency of the food.

Cheese is a common source of unwanted fat. Many cheeses are available in reduced-fat or nonfat varieties, but keep in mind that these varieties often don't melt as well. Another easy way to reduce the amount of fat added by cheese is simply to use less of it! Other dairy products, such as milk, sour cream, and mayonnaise, also show up often in Russian cooking. An easy way to trim fat from a recipe is to use skim or evaporated skim milk in place of cream, whole milk, or 2 percent milk. In recipes that call for sour cream or mayonnaise, try substituting low-fat or nonfat varieties, or plain yogurt.

When cooking with meat, buying extra-lean meats and trimming off as much fat as possible are two simple ways to reduce fat. In recipes that call for ground beef, some cooks like to substitute ground turkey to lower fat. However, since this does change the flavor, you may need to experiment a little bit to decide if you like this substitution.

There are many ways to prepare meals that are good for you and still taste great. As you become a more experienced cook, try experimenting with recipes and substitutions to find the methods that work best for you.

METRIC CONVERSIONS

Cooks in the United States measure both liquid and solid ingredients using standard containers based on the 8-ounce cup and the tablespoon. These measurements are based on volume, while the metric system of measurement is based on both weight (for solids) and volume (for liquids). To convert from U.S. fluid tablespoons, ounces, quarts, and so forth to metric liters is a straightforward conversion, using the chart below. However, since solids have different weights—one cup of rice does not weigh the same as one cup of grated cheese, for example—many cooks who use the metric system have kitchen scales to weigh different ingredients. The chart below will give you a good starting point for basic conversions to the metric system.

MASS (weight)

1 ounce (oz.)	=	28.0 grams (g)
8 ounces	=	227.0 grams
1 pound (lb.) or 16 ounces	=	0.45 kilograms (kg)
2.2 pounds	=	1.0 kilogram

LIQUID VOLUME

1 teaspoon (tsp.)	=	5.0 milliliters (ml)
1 tablespoon (tbsp.)	=	15.0 milliliters
1 fluid ounce (oz.)	=	30.0 milliliters
1 cup (c.)	=	240 milliliters
1 pint (pt.)	=	480 milliliters
1 quart (qt.)	=	0.95 liters (l)
1 gallon (gal.)	=	3.80 liters

LENGTH

¼ inch (in.)	=	0.6 centimeters (cm)
½ inch	=	1.25 centimeters
1 inch	=	2.5 centimeters

TEMPERATURE

212°F	=	100°C (boiling point of water)
225°F	=	110°C
250°F	=	120°C
275°F	=	135°C
300°F	=	150°C
325°F	=	160°C
350°F	=	180°C
375°F	=	190°C
400°F	=	200°C

(To convert temperature in Fahrenheit to Celsius, subtract 32 and multiply by .56)

PAN SIZES

8-inch cake pan	=	20 x 4-centimeter cake pan
9-inch cake pan	=	23 x 3.5-centimeter cake pan
11 x 7-inch baking pan	=	28 x 18-centimeter baking pan
13 x 9-inch baking pan	=	32.5 x 23-centimeter baking pan
9 x 5-inch loaf pan	=	23 x 13-centimeter loaf pan
2-quart casserole	=	2-liter casserole

A Russian Table

The table and the stove are two of the most important fixtures of any Russian home. In a rural dwelling, the stove may fill up a large part of the family's main room, where it serves as a source of warmth, light, and, of course, food. The table occupies a central spot of its own and is usually set for a meal with a linen cloth, silverware, small plates and glasses, and sometimes fresh flowers or greenery. If zakuski (appetizers) are being served, the table is also covered with a tempting array of dishes to whet the appetite.

To Russians, the most important part of the dinner table is the guests around it. Traditionally, every visitor is offered bread and salt, two items that even the most modest household is rarely without. In fact, the Russian word for hospitality, *khlebosol'stvo*, comes from the words for bread (*khleb*) and salt (*sol*). Russians are famous for their great hospitality, and no guest is ever turned away, no matter how crowded the table. No one ever leaves hungry, either, as a Russian host or hostess sees to it that everyone enjoys a full meal.

This Russian family gathers around an Easter table adorned with fresh flowers and colorfully dyed eggs.

A Russian Menu

The following menus are examples of a typical Russian dinner and supper. Shopping lists of the ingredients necessary to prepare these meals are also included. Keep in mind that these combinations of dishes are just suggestions. You can make your own menu plans based on the available ingredients, the occasion, and the amount of time that you have to prepare.

DINNER

Appetizers

Beet soup

Spring vegetable salad

Boiled potatoes

Beef Stroganoff

Tea

SHOPPING LIST:

Produce

1 pint cherry tomatoes
4 cucumbers
2 carrots
1 green pepper
1 head cabbage
2 beets
2 lb. new potatoes
3 medium potatoes
3 bunches radishes
6 onions
1 bunch scallions
1 bunch fresh parsley
1 head garlic
1 lemon

Dairy/Egg/Meat

8 oz. feta cheese
assorted cheeses, sliced or cut into wedges
32 oz. sour cream
2 sticks butter or margarine
1½ lb. beef (such as sirloin or tips)
½ lb. herring (smoked or pickled)
½ lb. chopped liver
12 slices assorted cold cuts

Canned/Bottled/Boxed

1 small jar dill pickles
1 small jar marinated mushrooms or other vegetable
4 28-oz. cans beef broth (or 1 jar beef bouillon cubes)
16 oz. tomato juice
lemon juice
sunflower oil
olive oil

Miscellaneous

1 package party rye bread
black tea, loose or in teabags
flour
dry mustard
fresh or dried dill
salt
pepper
sugar cubes

SUPPER

Cheese pancakes

Russian salad

Raspberry kisel

Produce

6 large potatoes
1 onion
1 bunch scallions
1 bunch fresh parsley
1 lb. raspberries (fresh or
   frozen)

Dairy/Egg/Meat

2 lb. farmer cheese or ricotta
   cheese
8 oz. mayonnaise
8 oz. sour cream
8 oz. whipping cream (or 1
   container prepared
   whipped cream)
7 eggs
2 skinned, boneless chicken
   breasts

Canned/Bottled/Boxed

1 small jar dill pickles
1 16-oz. can sweet peas
sunflower oil
olive oil
cornstarch

Miscellaneous

flour
sugar
fresh or dried dill
salt
pepper

Breakfast / Zavtrak

The first meal of the day is very important to Russians, especially to those who live in the countryside. Many people in Russia live in cold climates or perform difficult outdoor work. Usually a simple but filling meal, breakfast provides energy for the first and most productive part of the day. During the week, breakfast is usually eaten at about 8:00 A.M.

Sunday breakfast, or *voskresenye zavtrak*, is different than breakfasts during the week. On Sundays, Russians usually eat breakfast between 9:00 and 10:00 A.M. It is a bigger and heavier meal than a weekday breakfast, and all members of the family look forward to it as a time to be together.

Serve a hearty breakfast of sausage (bottom), potatoes with dressing (top left), and fresh rye bread (top right). (Recipes on pages 32–33, 34, and 35.)

Rye Bread / Rzhanoi Khleb

Russia is known the world over for its wonderful rye bread. This recipe makes a delicious, dense loaf that is well worth the time and the effort that it takes to make it.*

2 packages active dry yeast (4½ tsp.)

1 c. warm water (105°F to 115°F)

⅓ c. dark corn syrup

4½ to 5½ c. dark rye flour

2 tsp. salt

*The secret to making good rye bread is not to add too much flour and to be patient enough to let the dough rise fully.

1. In a large bowl, dissolve yeast in 1 c. warm water. Stir in corn syrup and set aside for 5 minutes, or until yeast mixture foams. If, after 5 minutes, yeast mixture has not started to foam, the water is too cold or too hot or the yeast is too old. Discard the yeast mixture and try again.

2. Add 2½ c. flour to yeast mixture, a little at a time, and beat with a spoon until smooth. Stir in salt.

3. Set bowl in a warm place, cover with a cloth towel (not terry cloth), and let rise for 30 minutes.

4. Add 2 to 3 more cups flour, ½ c. at a time, stirring after each addition. When dough becomes difficult to stir, turn out onto a floured surface and knead with your hands. Continue to add flour gradually until dough is stiff but still slightly sticky. Form dough into a ball.

5. Wash and dry bowl. Place dough in bowl, cover with a cloth towel that has been lightly dampened with warm water, and set in a warm place. Let rise for 2½ to 3 hours, or until dough almost doubles in size.

6. Turn dough out onto floured surface and, with floured hands, form into a loaf. Place loaf in a well-greased 9 × 5-inch baking pan, cover tightly with plastic wrap, and return to a warm place to rise for 1 hour.

7. Preheat oven to 350°F.

8. Bake loaf for 30 to 35 minutes. (Bread will not brown much.)

Preparation time: 45 minutes
(plus rising time of 4 to 4½ hours)
Baking time: 30 to 35 minutes
Makes 1 loaf

Potatoes with Dressing/Kartoshka v Mundire

While some foods are difficult to find in parts of Russia and may be expensive, potatoes are always available, and Russian cooks have found many ways to use them. Kartoshka v mundire* are often served for breakfast but make a simple side dish for any meal.

8 medium potatoes

1 tsp. salt

Dressing:

2 tbsp. vinegar

½ tsp. salt

⅛ tsp. pepper

⅓ c. sunflower oil

1. Scrub potatoes thoroughly, place in a large saucepan, and cover with water.

2. Bring water to a boil over high heat. Add salt, reduce heat to medium-low, and cover, leaving cover slightly ajar so steam can escape. Cook for 20 to 30 minutes, or until potatoes can be easily pierced with a fork.

3. While potatoes are cooking, prepare dressing. In a medium bowl, combine all ingredients except oil. Mix well with a whisk. Slowly add oil, beating constantly with whisk. Set aside.

4. Drain potatoes in a colander and set aside until cool enough to handle. Peel potatoes, toss with vinegar and oil dressing. Serve warm or at room temperature.

*Because these potatoes are cooked first and then peeled, their name literally means "potatoes in their jackets."

Preparation time: 10 minutes
Cooking time: 25 to 35 minutes
Serves 4 to 6

Sausage / Sardelka

Beef or pork sausage is a simple dish that is a favorite for breakfast but can be served at any meal as an appetizer, side dish, or even main course. It is very popular because it makes an inexpensive and filling meal. For a low-fat alternative, try chicken or turkey sausage.

1 lb. smoked, precooked beef or pork sausage (such as kielbasa)

1. Place sausage in a large saucepan and cover with water.

2. Bring water to a boil over medium-high heat. Boil for 5 to 7 minutes, or until meat is heated through. Serve hot with mustard.*

Preparation and cooking time: 10 to 15 minutes
Serves 4

*Russians like their mustard hot. To prepare typical Russian-style mustard, combine 4 tbsp. dry mustard with 2 tsp. water in a small bowl and mix well to make a paste. Carefully pour 6 tbsp. boiling water over the paste. Set aside for 15 minutes. Pour off extra water. Stir in 3 tsp. fresh lemon juice, 1 tsp. vegetable oil, 3 tbsp. sugar, and a pinch of salt. Mix until smooth, and refrigerate. Be careful—a little bit of this flavorful blend goes a long way!

Dinner / Obed

Dinner, the main meal of the day in most Russian households, is usually eaten between 12:00 and 2:00 P.M. It is a large meal consisting of three to four courses and typically begins with zakuski (appetizers). Although the name *zakuski* actually means "little bites" in Russian, this first course can be quite filling. After the appetizers, a soup such as borsch or bouillon is usually served. This is followed by a main course of beef, pork, chicken, or fish, and one or more side dishes of potatoes, noodles, rice, or buckwheat. *Kompot*, a sweet fruit beverage, often concludes the meal. Diners may also enjoy tea as they sit around the table and chat after eating.

Pirozhki (bottom) make a tasty dinner with hot borsch (top right) *and crunchy spring vegetable salad (top left). (Recipes on pages 40, 41, and 44–45.)*

Appetizers / Zakuski

In Russia, the tradition of starting dinner with an appetizer may have begun in the countryside, where people had to travel great distances to visit each other. Hosts would serve substantial zakuski to their guests until everyone had arrived and dinner was served.

½ lb. herring, smoked or pickled

½ lb. chopped liver

12 slices assorted cold cuts

various cheeses, cut in thin wedges
   or slices

1 cucumber, sliced

12 cherry tomatoes

12 radishes, sliced

12 dill pickles

12 marinated mushrooms or other
   vegetables

1 package party rye bread

butter

Arrange all ingredients* attractively in an assortment of small dishes and bowls.

Preparation time: 10 minutes
Serves 4 to 6

These are just a few of the many items that you may choose to serve as zakuski. Be creative and come up with favorites of your own!

A delicious array of zakuski is sure to tempt hungry diners.

Beet Soup / Borsch

2 beets

2 carrots

2 onions, peeled

12 c. (3 qt.) beef broth, or 12 c.
    water with beef bouillon cubes*

3 medium potatoes

¼ head cabbage

¼ green pepper

1 bunch fresh parsley or 1 tbsp.
    dried parsley flakes

¼ tsp. salt

2 c. tomato juice

1 tsp. lemon juice

pepper to taste

sour cream and dill to garnish

*To make a completely vegetarian borsch,
use vegetable broth instead of beef broth.
Or, to make a heartier meat borsch,
brown ½ to 1 lb. sliced beef brisket or
tips and add to the broth in Step 5.

1. Scrub beets and carrots. Cut one onion in half and place in a Dutch oven with beets and one carrot.

2. Add 11 c. beef broth (or 11 c. water with bouillon cubes) and bring to a boil. Reduce heat to medium and use a ladle or spoon to skim off foam that forms on surface. Cook for 20 to 25 minutes, or until vegetables are soft.

3. Remove vegetables from Dutch oven with tongs. Discard onion and set carrot and beets aside to cool.

4. Peel potatoes and cut into quarters. Slice cabbage and green pepper into strips. Peel and slice raw carrot.

5. Add potatoes, cabbage, green pepper, raw carrot, parsley, salt, and remaining 1 c. broth or water. Cook for 20 minutes. Stir in tomato juice and cook for 8 to 10 minutes.

6. Peel the beets and cooked carrot, grate or chop finely, and add to soup. Cook for 10 to 15 minutes.

7. Add lemon juice and pepper before serving. If you used fresh parsley, remove and discard. Serve hot with sour cream and dill.

Preparation time: 10 minutes
Cooking time: 1¼ to 1¾ hours
Serves 6

Spring Vegetable Salad / *Ovoshnoy Salat Vesna*

Vegetable salad goes well with a variety of dressings. This recipe is made with sour cream, but it is also delicious when made with mayonnaise or with vinegar and oil.

2 bunches radishes

1 bunch scallions

3 cucumbers, peeled

8 oz. feta cheese

1 tbsp. olive oil

1½ c. sour cream*

½ tsp. salt

1. Wash vegetables well in cold water. Cut roots and leaves off of radishes. Cut roots and any dried-out tips off of scallions.

2. Slice cucumbers and radishes into thin rounds. Cut cheese into ¼-inch cubes. Chop scallions finely.

3. In a large bowl, combine oil, sour cream, and salt. Add vegetables and cheese and toss well. Serve at room temperature, or chill if desired.

Preparation time: 15 minutes
Serves 4 to 6

*To reduce the fat content of this creamy salad, substitute nonfat for regular sour cream or try strained nonfat yogurt. To strain yogurt, place a filter in a funnel over a jar. Spoon yogurt into the filter and place in the refrigerator. Allow the liquid to drip into the jar until yogurt is the consistency of sour cream.

Beet Salad / Vinegret

Vinegret is an old Russian recipe that is easy and inexpensive to prepare and very nutritious.

Salad:

3 medium beets

6 medium potatoes

3 medium carrots, peeled and
    chopped into short sticks

6 dill pickles

I medium onion, peeled

½ c. sauerkraut (optional)

Dressing:

⅓ c. olive oil

2 tbsp. red wine vinegar

I tsp. dry mustard

¼ tsp. salt

¼ tsp. pepper

chopped parsley or dill for garnish

1. Scrub beets, potatoes, and carrots and place in three separate saucepans. Add enough water to each pan to cover vegetables. Bring to a boil over high heat. Reduce heat to medium-low and cover, leaving lids slightly ajar so steam can escape. Cook for 15 to 25 minutes, or until vegetables can be easily pierced with a fork. (Carrots and potatoes will cook more quickly than beets.)

2. Drain vegetables in a colander and rinse with cold water until cool.

3. Cut pickles lengthwise into quarters, then chop into shorter wedges or sticks. Peel potatoes and beets and cut into ¼-inch cubes. Cut onion in half and slice thinly. Combine vegetables in a large bowl, add sauerkraut if desired, and mix well.

4. To make dressing, combine oil, vinegar, mustard, salt, and pepper in a small bowl. Beat with a whisk for 2 minutes. Pour dressing over vegetables and mix well. Garnish with chopped parsley or dill.

Preparation time: 30 to 35 minutes
Cooking time: 25 to 35 minutes
Serves 6 to 8

Stuffed Pastries/ *Pirozhki*

This traditional Russian dish can be served with the zakuski or as a main course. Pirozhki also make a favorite holiday treat.

Filling:

4 tbsp. sunflower oil

3 medium onions, peeled and chopped

1½ lb. lean ground beef*

1 tsp. salt

⅛ tsp. pepper

Dough:

2 c. all-purpose flour

⅛ tsp. salt

1 egg

½ to ¾ c. water or skim milk

melted butter (optional)

1. In a large frying pan, heat 2 tbsp. oil over medium-high heat for 1 minute. Add onions and sauté for about 5 to 10 minutes, or until golden brown. Remove from pan and set aside.

2. Add remaining 2 tbsp. oil to pan and heat for 1 minute over medium-high heat. Add meat and cook until brown, breaking meat into small pieces with a spatula or wooden spoon. Carefully drain off fat.

3. Place onions, meat, salt, and pepper in a blender or food processor. Cover and blend on maximum speed for 5 to 7 seconds. (If you don't have a blender, place ingredients in a large bowl and mash well with a fork.) Set filling aside.

4. To make dough, mix flour, salt, and egg in a medium bowl. Stir in water or milk, a little at a time, until dough is stiff.

*Pirozhki can also be stuffed with many vegetarian ingredients. Try substituting cooked cabbage, potatoes, or rice for the ground beef in this recipe.

5. Knead dough for 2 to 4 minutes on a floured surface. You may need to add more flour if dough is too sticky. Roll out dough to ⅛-inch thickness with a rolling pin. With a glass or a circular cookie cutter, cut out rounds of dough about 3 inches in diameter.

6. Preheat oven to 400°F.

7. Put 1 tbsp. filling on one half of a dough circle. Lightly dampen edges of dough with a little water. Fold dough over filling and press edges together first with your fingers, then with the tines of a fork. Repeat with remaining filling and dough.

8. Place pirozhki on a greased cookie sheet and bake for 30 minutes, or until golden brown. If desired, brush lightly with melted butter. Serve at room temperature.

Preparation time: 40 to 45 minutes
Cooking time: 45 minutes
Makes 12 to 18 pirozhki

Beef Stroganoff/Bef Stroganov

Beef Stroganoff, a dish that originated in the 1800s, was named after a member of an aristocratic Russian family.

3 tbsp. sunflower oil

3 medium onions, peeled and chopped

1½ lb. beef (filet, tips, or tenderloin), sliced in short, thin strips

1 pinch salt

1 pinch pepper

2 tbsp. butter

2 tbsp. flour

1 tsp. ground dry mustard

1 c. beef broth (or water with bouillon)

¼ c. sour cream

fresh parsley to garnish

1. Heat oil in a Dutch oven over medium-high heat for 1 minute. Add onions and sauté, stirring frequently, until golden brown.

2. Add beef, cover, and cook for 5 minutes over medium heat. Remove cover and sauté for another 5 minutes, or until meat is cooked through. Add salt and pepper, stir, and remove from heat.

3. Melt butter in a small saucepan. Add flour and dry mustard and beat mixture with a wire whisk. Cook for one minute, then gradually add beef broth. Stir constantly until sauce is fairly thick.

4. Add sour cream, mix well, and pour sauce over meat and onion mixture. Heat through, being careful not to boil. Garnish with sprigs of fresh parsley and serve hot.*

Preparation time: 10 minutes
Cooking time: 30 to 40 minutes
Serves 4 to 6

*Try serving "straw potatoes" with beef Stroganoff. Wash and peel four potatoes. Cut into long thin strips. Pour about one inch of oil into a large frying pan. Heat over medium heat. Place potatoes in oil with a slotted spoon. Fry for 10 to 12 minutes, stirring gently. When potatoes are golden, remove with a slotted spoon and drain on paper towels. Serve hot.

Tea / *Chai*

Tea is a favorite beverage in Russia. It may be drunk at any time of day, and it is always offered to guests. Most households have samovars, metal urns that keep water hot for a steaming cup of fresh tea.

1 c. water per person

1 tsp. black tea leaves (or 1 teabag) for each 2 to 3 c. water

lemon slices

sugar cubes

1. In a teakettle or saucepan, bring water to a boil over high heat.

2. Rinse a teapot with hot tap water.

3. Place tea in teapot. Fill teapot three-quarters full of boiling water and let steep for 5 to 7 minutes. Add remaining water.

4. If you used teabags, remove them from teapot after steeping so the tea doesn't become too strong. If you used loose tea, strain tea through a filter. Serve hot with lemon and sugar.*

Preparation and cooking time: 15 to 20 minutes

*Many Russians enjoy mixing a small amount of jam or preserves into their tea as a sweetener. Another variation is substituting a thin slice of apple for the lemon.

Fruit Compote / *Kompot*

Kompot is a thick, sweet fruit drink that makes an excellent dessert or snack. Serve kompot in tall glasses with spoons for scooping up the fruit at the bottom.

1 lb. fruit*

6 c. water

½ c. to 2 c. sugar

1 whole cinnamon stick

⅛ tsp. nutmeg

1. Wash fruit in cold water and cut into small pieces. Remove all pits and inedible seeds.

2. Place fruit in a large kettle and add 6 c. water. Bring to a boil over high heat.

3. Reduce heat to low, add ½ c. sugar, and stir. Cover and simmer for 20 to 25 minutes.

4. Depending on the combination of fruits you have used, you may want to add more sugar. (Add sugar sparingly—if kompot tastes sweet when hot, it will taste even sweeter when cold.)

5. Add cinnamon stick and nutmeg and stir well. Simmer for another 10 minutes.

6. Remove cinnamon stick. Serve hot, or chill and serve cold.

You may use a single type of fruit or an assortment of fruit for kompot. Apples, pears, plums, and berries are all delicious choices.

Preparation time: 10 to 15 minutes
(plus 1 to 2 hours chilling time if serving cold)
Cooking time: 35 to 45 minutes
Serves 6

Supper / Uzhin

In Russia, supper is eaten between 6:00 and 8:00 P.M. It is usually the lightest meal of the day and sometimes consists of just one dish. However, when Russians eat supper at a restaurant or as guests in someone's home, the meal usually becomes a combination of dinner and supper. This single, larger meal may include appetizers, soup, and sometimes dessert. A social supper also usually lasts for a long time, as guests leisurely enjoy their food and some good conversation. As with the midday meal, many diners drink tea following the meal.

Fresh dill adds a distinctly Russian flavor to a supper of baked fish (bottom) *and boiled potatoes* (top). *(Recipes on pages 52 and 53.)*

Boiled Potatoes/*Otvarnaya Kartoshka*

This dish is one of dozens of ways to prepare potatoes Russian-style.

2 to 2½ lb. new potatoes, peeled

1 medium onion, peeled

½ tsp. salt

1 bunch dill, or 1 tbsp. dried dill weed

¼ c. butter, melted

1 clove garlic, minced (optional)

1. Wash potatoes and onion and cut onion in half. Place potatoes and onion in a large saucepan, cover with water, and add salt.

2. Bring water to a boil over high heat. Reduce heat to medium-low and cover, leaving cover slightly ajar so steam can escape. Cook potatoes for about 20 minutes, or until they can be easily pierced with a fork.

3. If using fresh dill, wash thoroughly in cold water and chop finely. Combine dill, melted butter, and garlic, and set aside.

4. When potatoes are cooked, drain in a colander and discard onion. Return potatoes to pan. Pour butter mixture over potatoes, cover pan tightly, and shake gently to coat. Serve hot.

Preparation time: 10 minutes
Cooking time: 20 to 25 minutes
Serves 4 to 6

Baked Fish / Zapechonaya Riba

Try serving this simple but delicious dish with boiled potatoes for a filling winter meal.

8 white fish fillets (such as cod, halibut, or flounder), fresh or frozen and thawed, about 2 lb.

salt and pepper to taste

3 tbsp. lemon juice

¾ to 1 c. flour

5 tbsp. unsalted butter

2 onions, peeled and sliced into rings

½ c. mayonnaise or sour cream*

½ c. grated Gruyère or white cheddar cheese*

chopped fresh dill to garnish

*To lower the fat content of this dish, use nonfat mayonnaise or sour cream and half the amount of cheese.

1. Preheat oven to 375°F.

2. Rinse fish fillets under cold water, rub with salt and pepper, and place in a shallow dish. Sprinkle lemon juice over fillets and set aside for 15 minutes.

3. Put flour in a shallow baking dish and roll fillets in flour to coat lightly. In a frying pan, melt 3 tbsp. of butter over medium heat. Fry each floured fillet for 3 to 4 minutes on each side, or until fish turns opaque. Place fish in a baking dish.

4. Wash and dry frying pan. Melt remaining 2 tbsp. butter over medium heat. Sauté onions for 5 to 10 minutes, or until golden.

5. Use a knife or rubber spatula to spread mayonnaise or sour cream over fish. Place onions on top and sprinkle cheese over all.

6. Place dish in oven and bake for 10 to 15 minutes, or until surface is browned and bubbly. Remove from oven, sprinkle with dill, and serve hot.

Preparation time: 10 minutes (plus 15 minutes marination)
Cooking time: 40 to 55 minutes
Serves 4 to 6

Russian Salad / Salat Olivie

*This gourmet dish was created by a French chef in a Moscow restaurant in the 1860s, and it is still a must-have at Russian parties.**

Salad:

2 skinned, boneless chicken breasts

1 medium onion, peeled

6 large potatoes

6 eggs

8 medium dill pickles

1 16-oz. can sweet peas, drained

parsley, scallions, and dill to garnish

1. Wash chicken in cold water. Cut onion in half. Place chicken and onion in large saucepan, cover with water, and bring to a boil over high heat.

2. Cover pan, reduce heat to low and simmer for 30 to 40 minutes, or until chicken is tender and white all the way through. Remove from heat and let chicken cool to room temperature in broth. Discard onion.

3. While chicken is cooking, wash potatoes well, place in a large saucepan, and cover with water. Bring to a boil over high heat. Reduce heat to medium-low and cover pan, leaving cover slightly ajar so steam can escape. Cook until potatoes can be easily pierced with a fork. Drain in a colander and rinse with cold water until cool.

4. While chicken and potatoes are cooking, place eggs in a large saucepan, cover with water, and bring to a boil over high heat. Remove from heat, cover pan, and let stand for 20 to 25 minutes. Rinse with cold water until cool.

5. Cool salad ingredients to room temperature before preparing salad. Cut chicken into bite-sized pieces. Peel potatoes and eggs. Cut potatoes, eggs, and pickles lengthwise into quarters, then chop into wedges. Place in a large bowl.

Dressing:

2 tbsp. olive oil

1 c. mayonnaise**

1 c. sour cream**

¼ tsp. salt

¼ tsp. pepper

1. Prepare dressing in a small bowl. Combine olive oil, mayonnaise, sour cream, salt, and pepper and mix well. Add dressing and sweet peas to salad and toss well.

2. Serve in a large bowl and garnish with fresh parsley, chopped scallions, and fresh or dried dill.

Preparation time: 25 to 30 minutes
Cooking time: 1 to 1½ hours
Serves 6 to 8

There are many variations on this old favorite. Some cooks add chopped apples or carrots. Or, to add some extra zing to your dressing, try adding about 1 tbsp. fresh lemon juice or Dijon mustard in Step 6.

**To lower the fat content of this traditional dish, use reduced-fat or nonfat varieties of mayonnaise and sour cream.*

Cheese Pancakes/ *Sirniki*

Sirniki can be eaten for supper or for breakfast. They are often served with sour cream, honey, or jam.

2 lb. farmer cheese or ricotta cheese

1 egg

½ c. sugar, plus extra for sprinkling

½ tsp. salt

1 to 1½ c. all-purpose flour

sunflower oil for frying

1. In a large bowl, mash cheese with a fork. Add egg and mix well. Stir in sugar and salt.

2. Add flour, a little at a time, until dough is firm enough to knead by hand. Continue adding flour and kneading until dough can be shaped easily with hands.

3. Dust hands with flour and scoop up a piece of dough about the size of a medium apple. Roll into a ball between palms and press to form a pancake about 1 inch thick. Make a batch of 3 or 4 before frying.

4. Pour a thin layer of oil into a large frying pan and heat over medium heat for 1 minute. Carefully place pancakes in pan with a spatula and fry for 3 to 4 minutes, or until bottoms are golden brown. Turn over and fry until second side turns golden brown. Remove and place on paper towels.

5. Continue making and frying sirniki, adding more oil to pan when necessary, until dough is used up. Sprinkle with sugar and serve.*

*For a special summertime treat, serve sirniki with fresh strawberries or raspberries.

Preparation time: 15 to 20 minutes
Cooking time: 45 to 60 minutes
Serves 6

Raspberry Kisel / Malinoviy Kisel

Kisel is a thick fruit dessert that is served chilled.

I lb. raspberries (fresh or frozen and thawed)*

½ c. cornstarch

8½ c. water

I c. sugar

whipped cream or nondairy topping

*Kisel can also be made with strawberries, blueberries, blackberries, cranberries, cherries, apricots, peaches, or plums.

1. If using fresh raspberries, wash in cold water and drain well. Place raspberries in a large bowl and crush well with the back of a spoon. Set aside.

2. In a small bowl, combine cornstarch with ½ c. water and stir until cornstarch is completely dissolved. Set aside.

3. In a large saucepan, combine sugar and remaining 8 c. water and stir well. Bring to a boil over high heat, stirring occasionally.

4. Add crushed fruit and cornstarch mixture to boiling syrup and stir for 4 to 8 minutes, or until mixture begins to thicken.

5. Remove pan from heat and let kisel cool to room temperature. Refrigerate for at least 2 hours and serve chilled in glasses. Top with whipped cream.

Preparation time: 10 minutes
(plus chilling time of at least 2 hours)
Cooking time: 10 to 20 minutes
Serves 6

Fresh raspberries make kisel a delectable summer treat.

Holiday and Festival Food

Many Russian holidays and festivals are strongly associated with certain foods. For example, Maslenitsa (Butter Week) just isn't the same without plenty of blini. During the chilly winter weather, Russians enjoy warm, fresh blini at home, buy them from street vendors, and even take part in blini-eating contests. But they also eat these delicious pancakes during the rest of the year. Similarly, kutya, a traditional Christmastime dish, makes a tasty and nutritious vegetarian meal no matter what the season. The holiday recipes in this chapter are perfect to prepare for your friends or family on a special occasion—and they just might become everyday favorites, as well.

Make your holiday table festive with a plate of sugary twig cookies. (Recipe on pages 68–69.)

Pancakes / Blini

Blini are a must during Maslenitsa, but they make a delicious breakfast on any day.

4 c. all-purpose flour

2 c. buttermilk

1 egg

½ tsp. salt

1 tbsp. sugar

½ to 1 c. warm water (optional)

sunflower oil for frying

* Serve blini with tasty toppings such as butter, sour cream, jam, fresh berries, ricotta cheese, smoked fish, or caviar.

1. Place flour in a large mixing bowl. Gradually add buttermilk, beating well with a spoon.

2. Add egg, salt, and sugar and stir until blended. Mixture should be the consistency of pancake batter. If mixture is too thick, stir in ½ c. warm water. Set batter in a warm place for 10 to 15 minutes.

3. Lightly grease a small frying pan with 1 tsp. oil. Heat pan for several seconds over medium heat. Pour ¼ c. batter into pan, quickly swirling pan so a thin, even layer covers the bottom. (If batter has thickened, add a little more warm water to mixture in bowl and beat well.) When edge of pancake lifts easily from pan (about 2 to 3 minutes), carefully flip over with a spatula.

4. When other side lifts easily from pan, remove pancake, place on a plate, and cover with a cloth towel. Repeat with remaining batter, adding more oil to the pan when necessary. Serve warm.

Preparation time: 25 to 30 minutes
Cooking time: 25 to 35 minutes total
Serves 4 to 6

Easter Sweet Bread/*Kulich*

Dough:

I package (¼ oz.) active dry yeast

¼ c. warm water

¼ c. sugar

½ c. warm milk

I c. flour

8 tbsp. unsalted butter

½ c. sugar

8 egg yolks (save 2 egg whites)*

I tsp. vanilla extract

2 tsp. ground cardamom

½ tsp. salt

3 to 3½ c. flour

⅓ c. golden raisins

¼ c. slivered almonds

¼ c. chopped candied orange rind
   (optional)

Glaze:

I c. powdered sugar

2 tsp. lemon juice

⅛ tsp. almond extract

2 to 3 tsp. warm water

1. In a large bowl, combine yeast, ¼ c. warm water, ¼ c. sugar, and warm milk. Stir until yeast and sugar have dissolved. Add 1 c. flour and stir until blended. Cover bowl with a towel and let stand in a warm place for one hour.

2. In another large bowl, combine butter, ½ c. sugar, and egg yolks. Add the yeast-flour mixture to butter mixture and stir well. Add vanilla extract, cardamom, salt, and enough flour to make a soft dough. Stir in raisins, almonds, and orange rind.

3. In a small bowl, use an electric beater to beat 2 egg whites until stiff. Carefully fold into dough. Turn dough onto a clean, lightly floured surface and knead gently for 5 minutes, or until dough is smooth and elastic. Place in a greased bowl and turn to grease all sides of dough. Cover with a towel and let rise in a warm place for 1½ to 2 hours, or until doubled in size.

4. Grease a clean, 2-lb. coffee can with butter or shortening and line the sides and bottom of the can with brown packaging paper or strips of a grocery bag. Use butter or margarine to grease the side of the paper that will be touching the dough so that

bread will not stick to paper. Make sure that the edges of the paper stick out over the top edge of the can by at least one inch. Fold paper down over outside of can.

5. Punch down dough and knead lightly. Place dough in coffee can. Cover with a towel and let rise for 45 to 60 minutes, or until dough reaches the top of the can.

6. Preheat oven to 400°F. Bake loaf for 10 minutes, then reduce heat to 350°F and bake for another 35 to 40 minutes, or until kulich is golden brown and a toothpick or cake tester inserted into the center of the top comes out clean.

7. While kulich is baking, prepare glaze. In a small bowl, combine powdered sugar, lemon juice, almond extract, and enough water to make a smooth glaze that is runny enough to be drizzled.

*To separate an egg, crack it cleanly on the edge of a nonplastic bowl. Holding the two halves of the eggshell over the bowl, gently pour the egg yolk back and forth between the two halves, letting the egg white drip into the bowl and being careful not to break the yolk. When most of the egg white has been separated, place the yolk in another bowl.

8. Remove kulich from oven and let cool for 10 minutes. Very carefully remove from can and cool on a rack. While kulich is still slightly warm, drizzle glaze over the top. Serve by cutting off crown and slicing base into rounds. Replace crown to keep bread moist.

Preparation time: 40 to 45 minutes
(plus 3½ to 4 hours rising time)
Cooking time: 45 to 55 minutes
Makes 1 loaf

Wheat Porridge / Kutya

Kutya is a traditional Christmas Eve dish in Russia and other former republics of the USSR.

1 c. wheat berries, whole*

4 c. water

¼ tsp. salt

½ c. poppy seeds

½ c. slivered almonds

⅓ c. honey

½ c. raisins

cinnamon for sprinkling

Look for wheat berries in the bulk foods or health section of your grocery store or in a specialty health-food grocery or co-op. If you don't find them, you can make a simpler version of kutya with cream of wheat. Boil 2 c. water, stir in 1 c. cream of wheat, and cook, stirring, until mixture thickens. Remove from heat and add other ingredients as directed in recipe above.

1. Place wheat berries in a large pan with enough cold water to cover. Soak overnight.

2. The next day, drain wheat berries and refill pan with 4 c. water. Stir in salt and bring to a boil. Reduce heat and simmer uncovered for 2 to 3 hours, or until wheat berries are tender. If water gets too low, add enough to cover wheat berries.

3. While wheat berries are cooking, soak poppy seeds in a small bowl of lukewarm water for 30 minutes. Drain seeds and grind in a food processor or coffee grinder. Set aside.

4. Preheat oven to 350°F. Spread almonds on a baking sheet and toast for 3 to 5 minutes, or until light gold. Set aside to cool.

5. When wheat berries are tender, drain and place in a large serving bowl. Stir in poppy seeds, honey, raisins, and two-thirds of toasted almonds. Mix well. Garnish with remaining almonds and sprinkle cinnamon over all. Serve warm.

Preparation time: 15 minutes (plus overnight soaking time)
Cooking time: 2 to 3 hours
Serves 6

Twig Cookies / Khvorost

Khvorost means "twigs" in Russian and refers to the shape and the crunchiness of these delicious little cookies. An old favorite, they are an especially popular treat for "name days." Each day of the Russian Orthodox calendar is associated with a saint, and people who share that saint's name celebrate their name day, much like a birthday.

2½ c. flour

2 egg yolks

1 egg

¼ c. whipping cream*

½ tsp. vanilla extract

1 tsp. non-alcoholic rum flavoring or rum extract

5 tsp. water

⅛ tsp. salt

½ c. powdered sugar

vegetable oil for frying

1. Place flour in a large mixing bowl. Form a hollow in the center and add egg yolks, egg, whipping cream, vanilla, rum flavoring, and water. Mix well.

2. Stir in salt and ¼ c. of the powdered sugar. Turn dough out onto a clean, lightly floured surface and knead until dough becomes smooth and pliable. Return half of the dough to the bowl and cover with a towel.

3. Use a floured rolling pin to roll the other half of the dough to a thickness of about ⅛ inch. Cut into strips 5 inches long and 1½ to 2 inches wide.

4. Use a sharp knife to cut a 2-inch slit lengthwise from the center toward one end of each strip. Thread the other end of the strip through the slit and twist slightly. Repeat with all remaining strips and repeat the process with the other half of the dough.

5. Place about one inch of oil in a deep kettle or frying pan and heat to 365°F (if you have a fat thermometer). If you don't have a fat thermometer, heat until a drop of water flicked into the pan jumps out.

6. Carefully place 3 or 4 twists of dough into oil and fry, turning once, for about 5 minutes, or until golden brown. Remove with a slotted spoon and drain on paper towels.

7. To serve, place cookies on a platter and sprinkle with remaining powdered sugar.

Preparation time: ¾ to 1¼ hours
Cooking time: 1 hour
Makes 3 to 4 dozen cookies

*To lower fat in this recipe, substitute evaporated skim milk for whipping cream.

Index

About the Authors

Gregory and Rita Plotkin were born in the former Soviet Union, where they both learned to love cooking the Russian way. After moving to the United States, Gregory and Rita continued to enjoy cooking their native cuisine and sharing it with their friends.

Photo Acknowledgments
The photographs in this book are reproduced courtesy of: © Trip/A. Tjagny-Rjadno, p. 2–3; © Walter and Louiseann Pietrowicz/September 8th Stock, p. 4 (both), 5 (both), 6, 18, 30, 36, 39, 42, 47, 50, 57, 58, 60, 63, 66; © Andrea Jemolo/Corbis, p. 10; © David and Peter Turnley/Corbis, p. 12; © Trip/B. Seed, pp. 15, 26; © Trip/I. Deineko, p. 17.

Cover Photos: © Walter and Louiseann Pietrowicz/September 8th Stock, front cover (both), spine, back cover.

The illustrations on pp. 7, 19, 27, 31, 32, 34, 35, 37, 38, 40, 41, 44, 46, 48, 49, 51, 53, 55, 56, 59, 61, 62, 65, 67, and 69 and the map on page 8 are by Tim Seeley.